Ric Charlesworth co: hockey team, the Hoc ranking in 1993, whe winning gold in two Olympic Games.

Voted 'Team Coach of the Year' six times, Ric has represented Australia as a hockey player in four Olympic Games and played for Western Australia in First Class cricket. He has been selected as Western Australia's greatest ever hockey player and also Western Australia's greatest ever coach. After graduating in medicine and practising as a doctor, he was a member of Federal Parliament for ten years. Ric spent a year living in Italy writing and consulting in Europe with teams from professional soccer and rugby. Ric has worked as High Performance Manager to New Zealand Cricket. He is now the Head Coach of the Australian Mens' Hockey team, the Kookaburras.

Staying at the Top was his second book. *The Coach: Managing for Success* was first published in 2001 and his third book *Shakespeare the Coach* was published in 2004.

Visit Ric's website:
www.riccharlesworth.com.au

STAYING AT THE TOP

RIC CHARLESWORTH

First published in 2002 in Pan
by Pan Macmillan Australia Pty Limited
St Martins Tower, 31 Market Street, Sydney

Reprinted 2002, 2009, 2011

National Library of Australia
Cataloguing-in-Publication data:

Charlesworth, Richard.
Staying at the top.

ISBN 0 330 36366 2.

1. Sports administration. 2. Coaching (Athletics).
3. Leadership. 4. Management, 5. Success, I. Title.

796.069

Cover photo supplied by Hockey Australia

Foreword

Successful teams and people take good ideas from wherever they can find them. Sport has much to teach those of us who make our way in the business world. Winning companies are successful teams. They succeed because they are cohesive and yet manage to get the best out of individuals who are their life blood.

I have always been struck by how much there is to learn from successful sporting teams, their players, coaches and managers. They have to compete globally, adapt quickly to new ideas and absorb new techniques. The whole team has to be geared towards getting to the top.

But if getting to the top is hard, staying there for any length of time is even harder. How do winning teams re-energise themselves over the years to prevent themselves from being pushed off the summit? Winning teams become the focus for all their competitors – their methods and strategies are examined in detail and quickly copied. Copying strategies is one thing, delivering the same result is quite another. It is here that leaders and coaches earn their keep.

So often it is the *way* things are done that makes the difference – ensuring that individuals are clear about how they can best contribute to team success. How is the next generation being developed to step up when the time comes? How well is that transition handled? How thoroughly is the opponent's game plan analysed? How quickly does the team react to unforeseen events in the heat of battle? Sporting teams and businesses alike are judged by how well they respond to these demanding challenges.

I've known Richard Charlesworth since we were at Christ Church Grammar School together in Perth in the mid 1960s. We shared a love of sport and a determination to win. We went on to play cricket together for the University of Western Australia. He combined international hockey and state cricket with his studies in medicine, which speaks to both his talents and his determination. He didn't drink in those days so at least he didn't waste too much time at the bar. He has since developed a love of good red wine which has rounded him out nicely.

My own sporting skills were a fraction of his so I realised I had to work hard, and focus on my own strengths and weaknesses if I was to make any progress. No one in our team was more focused than Richard and it was that, combined with his remarkable talents, that set him on the road to success.

I never found him selfish in his pursuit of victory. Insights were shared and success came from the team's performance – qualities essential to a great coach. Few great players become great coaches simply because they fail to understand how the rest of us cannot make the miraculous look commonplace – or if they do they cannot communicate it. Richard has learnt to do both and in doing so laid claim to being the most successful coach in Australian sporting history.

There are few certainties in life and success in our chosen field is not one of them. Richard Charlesworth knows how to turn the 'art of the possible' into the 'art of the probable' and dramatically increase the chances of getting to the top. His insights as a uniquely successful coach flow from the pages of *Staying at the Top*. They speak of the man and his methods, and are invaluable to us all.

Rod Eddington
Chief Executive
British Airways

Contents

Introduction

We all want to succeed, to do well, to be the best, to climb the mountain. Most of us are capable of doing something well, and unless we want to achieve in an area in which we have no ability or talent, then usually we can succeed. Many of us can be the best in our own little area of competence for a short while.

However, enduring champions – the really great champions – are rare. Sometimes teams and individuals consistently produce high-quality performances that make them exceptional. Businesses may set and maintain the industry

> **Most of us are capable of doing something well.**

standard in performance, sales, innovation, service etc. How do they do it?

Getting to the top and succeeding in what we want to do is only half the tale. Vigilance and a strategy for staying on top are equally important once you get there. Indeed, while achieving success you should be putting in place practices that will ensure continued success once you are there. It is not sufficient or desirable to focus narrowly on getting to the top without considering what will keep you there. This is not putting the cart before the horse as the adage goes, it is merely good and prudent practice.

In Part 1, I will endeavour to describe the ingredients central to realising your potential in your chosen field. What will enable you or your

> **It is not sufficient or desirable to focus narrowly on getting to the top without considering what will keep you there.**

group to be the best you can be – to climb the mountain? I will outline strategies useful in sport and describe situations analogous with business experiences.

In Part 2, I will deal with how to stay at the top once you have got there. In my book *The Coach: Managing for Success* I touched on this topic in the chapter entitled 'Chronic Achievement'. I described briefly some of the strategies that helped the Hockeyroos – the Australian women's hockey team, which I coached – maintain the quality of their performance during the four years that elapsed between their gold-medal win at the Olympics in Atlanta and the Sydney 2000 Olympics, where they also won gold. What I plan to do in this book is to explore what makes teams and individuals great and the attitudes, qualities and practices that underpin a sustained winning culture.

Whether the endeavour is as an individual or in a team, we all require the assistance of others to realise our potential. Co-operation and teamwork are part of any successful enterprise. No one is more aware of this than a team coach whose task is to select, train and prepare a group for the rigours of competition.

Our society tends to regard training and learning as merely the precursors of 'real' jobs and 'real' work. We think that learning is behind us once we are employed. The reality is much different. The best coaches of sporting teams know that perfect performances are usually the result of continuous polishing and practice and that the best players want input from coaches. The process of refining one's performance as an athlete is ongoing, and coaching is a continuous search for the best way to extend performances beyond what the athletes believe is possible.

> **Co-operation and teamwork are part of any successful enterprise.**

Athletes learn most by *doing*, and with good coaching their experience becomes one of continuous learning and growth. This, too, is the essence of an ever-growing organisation that remains at the cutting edge of innovation and improvement. Such organisations know that learning and training never end. They find that the outcomes look after themselves if they focus on the practices and processes of being the best they can be.

Wherever possible in this book I have tried to illustrate my arguments with examples from sport, literature or business. Additionally, I quizzed a number of Hockeyroos about how they were able to find their way through the

> **Athletes learn most by *doing*, and with good coaching their experience becomes one of continuous learning and growth.**

many and inevitable trials that beset those who dare to try to reach, then stay on the mountain top. I hope you will find their stories interesting.

Right from the beginning my aim with the Hockeyroos was to establish best practice and to be the best team in the world. When you set out on such a journey you never know if you will succeed, or, if you do, how long it will take. The fact that our team quite quickly established themselves reflects the fact that they had previously underperformed.

Once we were pre-eminent and began to win consistently, my goal was initially simply to continue to grow. Indeed, until we won in Atlanta I was still primarily interested in establishing the quality we wanted and pushing what I describe as my first five principles. (These are the first five principles described in Part 1.)

It was not until after Atlanta that I actively thought about staying at the top. In accepting another contract with the Hockeyroos which would take us to the Sydney Olympics together,

I took on what I believe is a coach's greatest challenge, that of maintaining prominence. I had to put my mind to dealing with the issues that bring teams down. These issues I believe, are the same ones that undermine businesses, and indeed any organisations, that are successful.

Out of my experiences and our battle to stay ahead of our opponents came the principles of *Staying at the Top*. But, again, I should emphasise that I did not spend four years concerned with the record or what it might look like. My focus, and hopefully that of the athletes, was on the details of everyday training and improvement. The outcome (four more years at the top) was achieved by attention to the process of being as good as we could be and doing everything possible to achieve that. The principles espoused in this book were seldom outside my field of vision during that time.

PART 1

The Five Principles of Being the Best

What are the five principles of being the best? For me they are:

- quality
- teamwork
- learning and training
- resilience
- depth and flexibility.

These principles are the essence of what I tried to establish in the Hockeyroos' program. Some people will suggest that having defined, specific goals ought to be one of the first principles mentioned in any list of how to be the best. They will be surprised it is not on my list. I would argue, rather, that in building a substantial winning program, the emphasis must be on the detail of improving every athlete every day. The team goals and athlete goals, which we set, could never be achieved without doing this. Then, the outcome looks after itself. The outcome of being the best is a given.

What the Hockeyroos achieved in being number one for eight consecutive years, winning consecutive World Cups and consecutive Olympic gold medals was never our goal. In 1993, I never would have believed that possible! Certainly, the athletes and I, and the rest of the Hockeyroo staff, dreamed of winning major championships, and set out to do so, but we only achieved our record by paying attention to the everyday details of our sport.

Let's look now at the principles in a general way, before examining them one by one.

If you are in business, you probably would agree that it is easier to market and sell a **quality product** than one of a lower standard. Similarly, **quality service** keeps customers happy! Sport is no different. While there will be aberrations in performance, over time the best quality athletes and teams will win most of the time.

The Olympic Games, because they are held only once every four years, provide many examples of such aberrations. World champions or world record-holders only win gold at the Olympics every three or four events. Across all sports, this is a fairly consistent outcome. My aim as a coach was to try to build a margin for error in my team that could overcome the vagaries of competition at that level. I believed this could only be done by an uncompromising push for quality in every aspect of our approach.

I wanted gifted, quality athletes. We had to work on building their fitness, skills and techniques. We would make them tactically superior; we would know our opponents better than anyone else. We would have the best **teamwork**, **depth** and **flexibility**, which would be honed in the harsh glare of competition. The competition, both internal (for places in the team) and external (from our opponents), would help to build a **resilient group** capable of handling any threat from any foe.

Tactics and strategy are as important in business as they are in sport but they can only work for you if you have skilled personnel putting them into practice. In the end your opponents must be given credit for knowing what they are doing, and so often the only difference in the performance of rival companies isn't the game plan, but the execution of it. Coaching and managing starts and finishes with preparing the athletes or staff as thoroughly as possible for the rigours of competition.

In the following pages I will endeavour to describe what I believe are some of the crucial elements of that preparation. A focus on quality and the building of teamwork, resilience, depth and flexibility occur best in an environment in which continual learning is valued and quality training is a core expectation.

> **Coaching and managing starts and finishes with preparing the athletes or staff as thoroughly as possible for the rigours of competition.**

It is in some ways artificial to separate these things into individual categories. Inevitably they overlap within any organisation or endeavour. However, in separating them into five principles I hope to provide some useful building blocks for you to apply to your own team or organisation.

These five principles, in my view, are the crucial elements that can ensure your team or organisation is the best.

1 Quality – Values, People and Practices

If the Hockeyroos remember anything from my time as coach, they will remember my pleas for thoroughness in all that we did. Thoroughness ensures attention to detail, a pursuit of excellence and an obsession with getting things right.

> **Thoroughness ensures attention to detail, a pursuit of excellence and an obsession with getting things right.**

Quality all the time in all you can do is not an option; it is a necessity if you want to be the best. You must know it, expect it, train it, select it and never accept less.

The coach must take responsibility for quality control in all the areas that affect the outcome for the athlete or team. In the same way the business leader or manager has responsibility for quality in the work environment.

In any organisation the crucial elements in performance are the processes and the people. If the processes are good but the staff or team cannot execute the tasks, the endeavour will fail. Similarly, good people with poor processes, tactics or systems will not be able to get the job done efficiently. Let's look at the practices of business and sport and compare them in some of these areas.

Quality values

The core values of the group or organisation underpin how you go about your business. From the beginning the Hockeyroos undertook to: never claim an illegitimate goal or advantage; always respect our opponents; to share the load; to work hard at learning about ourselves and the game; and to never give in.

These core values were aspired to by all and were the thread that held our program together. Every organisation, team, club or group should take the time to clarify and identify its core values. That time is time well spent.

Select quality

Perhaps some of the most difficult times for me as a coach occurred when we were selecting teams for the Olympics or World Championships. At such times many hours were spent deliberating

---

Every organisation, team, club or group should take the time to clarify and identify its core values.

---

over permutations and combinations of players. In addition, each player was individually assessed and her weaknesses and strengths were considered. She would usually have been through extensive periods of training and preparation before she was asked to perform. The selectors would make informed – though always difficult – choices, based on a wealth of information. Is this the norm in business? I suspect it usually is not. An interview and a few tests usually suffice. Perhaps the interviewers check on 'past form' with a referee or two. Some training might be offered when the successful candidate starts work, but there is usually little ongoing mentoring or coaching. An investment in the selection process and the search for quality among candidates are essential if good squads and teams are to be

> **Do we know enough about those we select to become part of our organisation?**

assembled. Do we know enough about those we select to become part of our organisation? I suspect not. Clearly, time spent in recruiting and selecting well is time productively utilised. A drawn-out selection process might be difficult to establish but one solution is employing for trial periods which allow for more thorough assessment of an individual's capabilities.

Finally, always try to be objective about the offerings of youth (potential and enthusiasm), compared with those of experience (past performance and competence). The balance of each of these categories is important for your team to function optimally. The best teams have a balance of both.

Train for quality

Ongoing coaching and assessment underpins quality performances.

Too many businesses, I fear, do not spend enough time doing on-the-job training to ensure quality practices under pressure in work situations. In sport, team and individual coaches are continually manufacturing game-like situations in which skills, techniques and tactics are honed. Additionally, the Hockeyroos had a program of approximately thirty international matches per year, of which most were seen as opportunities to provide the highest quality game experience. Usually in any given year the majority of these matches were not in major competitions and thus were seen as training and preparation for major competitions.

Learning is not something that occurs only at a university or college before we start work. It is an ongoing process that improves skills and practices, and develops awareness of tactics. All these things are part of the quest to become the best. Without

---

Learning is not something that occurs only at a university or college before we start work.

---

the challenge of non-stop learning, employees stagnate and are often without direction.

Employers and managers in business should see their employees as athletes and train them to perform. Analysis of performance, correction of errors, researching opponents and teaching skills are all part of the employer's thorough approach to quality in all they do.

Equally important to skill and tactical training are physical capacities and mental and emotional resources. Most training for business performance tends to focus on cognitive or mental skill training. The sports coach, however, must work on all three – physical, emotional, and mental and cognitive training.

Coaches learn quickly that an athlete's emotional environment and resources can be crucial,

---

Employers and managers in business should see their employees as athletes and train them to perform.

---

and, of course, physical conditions impact crucially on sports performance. Very few managers in business are aware of overtraining or the need for adequate rest or appropriate diet in their employees. These areas of business management are largely untapped.

Coaches in sport are intimately involved in making sure their athletes are physically and emotionally prepared. Business, I suspect, can learn much in this area.

Know quality

When selecting athletes for a team, coaches know the sort of competencies they require. Some things can be taught and developed. Most elite athletes can make improvements in technique with practice and supervision. Most learn a great deal about game strategy and tactics once in the elite team. However, those without speed can only be improved at the margin. Speed was always something that I selected for. No one ever made a slow athlete fast, but athletes who are technically and tactically deficient can be significantly improved.

So selections in sport are made with knowledge of what is required and what the athlete can offer. I wonder whether this always occurs in business? Each business will be different but the competent manager must know what is essential, what is preferable and what can be developed in the business. Those providing services and dealing with the public would value good communication more than someone requiring great manual dexterity to manufacture a precision instrument or the concentration to crunch numbers on a computer.

When choosing a team, as a coach I always preferred, all else being equal, athletes with open

> **The competent manager must know what is essential, what is preferable and what can be developed in the business.**

minds to those who were negative in their attitude to change and development. In business, too, willingness to adapt and embrace change is essential. Let's look at the story of Tom O'Toole, Australia's most famous baker. He turned his failing bakery in Beechworth in country Victoria into a multi-million-dollar business employing over fifty people by using commonsense and enthusiasm. Now he is a much sought-after motivational speaker. He selected his staff for their attitude, and trained them in the necessary skills. As a coach or manager you should look for the raw materials and the will to be good. If you start with those you are well on the way to success.

Not many of us are extremely gifted or exceptionally talented in any area of endeavour. Genius is as rare in sport as it is in music, art,

> **As a coach or manager you should look for the raw materials and the will to be good.**

science or business. Mostly what carries us through is the drive to do something really well. We set up a routine of practices and habits that enables us to utilise our talents to the utmost. Those who may be more naturally gifted but without those practices and habits may start well, but will not endure.

Propagate quality

The job of the coach or manager is to oversee people and processes objectively and critically. In sport, this occurs at training and 'on the job' in matches. Through rewarding, reprimanding and redirecting appropriately and consistently you establish the habit of quality performance.

Through rewarding, reprimanding and redirecting appropriately and consistently you establish the habit of quality performance.

Coaches prepare the team, oversee the game and have the capacity to influence part of the contest. In business, many managers spend too little time on preparation of their staff and then try to run the game from the top. Similarly many coaches interfere too much in the game in progress to the detriment of their team. Mostly once the game is underway the coach can only tinker at the edges of a contest. The important work occurs in preparation and training, and then in providing support and feedback once in the contest. Your employees need to be prepared and supplied with the right resources, and then need support and feedback on a continuous basis in order to perform.

Most of this chapter has been about what

> **The important work occurs in preparation and training, and then in providing support and feedback once in the contest.**

coaches do. An absolutely indispensable part of team development is what the players do. As mentors for other players they can provide the best example, the best leadership, the best teaching of anyone in the group. I was fortunate to inherit a team that was willing to work hard (and for this I give full credit to my predecessor as coach). What we were able to add to this culture of diligence was a culture of quality and enterprise in which innovation and learning were crucial values. Hence, the team taught the team; individuals advised individuals; and the values, behaviours and techniques taught by the coaches were propagated by the players among the group as they helped each other improve. In such an environment, quality flourishes and is a vital force.

In most workplaces one spends most of one's time with colleagues of similar status rather than with management. Hence the advice, ideas, support and teaching of senior colleagues is crucial to propagating the values and practices which ensure quality. While management should ensure that good practice is in place it cannot do all of the coaching, much of which occurs at a colleague to colleague level. Mentoring to propagate the company's values and practices is critical for your business to be awash with quality.

The art of coaching is to get that balance between coach and players right, and the same art is required in business. The staff must be able to do their jobs while the boss oversees and finesses progress. The coach has a crucial role in ensuring that the players can reproduce their skills under pressure, make good decisions and judgments and fix problems that may arise.

Some tips for establishing quality

1 Establish a quality culture by not accepting second best or compromising. When things are done sloppily or people cut corners make sure that everyone understands that such practices are not acceptable. Do this right from the start and be consistent and firm without being overcritical or deprecatory.

2 Once the culture is sound, encourage and support mentoring within the group, both formally and informally. Over time you will have a system that continuously reinforces the values and behaviours required.

3 Ignore youth at your peril – being new or young doesn't exclude quality. Experience can be overrated; however, it is also important to give everyone opportunities to show what they can do. Older players or those who are late developers should be assessed principally on performance, present competence and perhaps a recent record of willingness to learn and develop.

4 Make the selection process for your team or organisation as rigorous as possible. Remember that impressions formed over one or two days can change in a week, so give yourself time to ruminate and flush out foibles. One solution is to employ initially for a trial period on probation.

5 Select those who want it most – those with positive attitudes who are willing to learn – along with those with the best skills. Some of each category will fall by the wayside but many will surprise you.

6 Train those you select in every area – physically, emotionally and mentally. You need rounded, balanced individuals to build a successful team or workforce.

7 Aim to be 20 per cent better than the industry standard or the opposition, whichever is the higher. The aim should never just be to get the next win or next contract. You need to aim beyond that and then immerse yourself in the detail. The next contest will look after itself and be placed in perspective by the larger vision.

8 Having taken on the best people, make sure that the practices and processes are right. Scour the systems and require that the highest quality control be in place. Good people will help you fix any weaknesses in their practices and vice versa.

9 The mantra of **quality** must underpin all you do.

2 Teamwork

What do we mean by this term – teamwork –
that glibly slips from our lips but in fact does not
come naturally to many of us? Most athletes, for
example, have a healthy degree of self-interest,
as do ambitious employees in any organisation.
Tolerance, sharing, selflessness and thinking
about others aren't always the most natural inclinations. They must be conceived as part of the
team or workplace culture, developed and
worked on. The word 'teamwork' says it all – it
is challenging and difficult to be a good *team*;
you have to *work* at it. Coaches and managers
play a central role in establishing an environment that encourages and rewards this 'work'.

It takes time to develop a sense of team in an organisation. One of the most difficult tasks in coaching a national sporting team was having a group of more than twenty-five athletes of whom only sixteen would be selected for the main competitions. Internal competition for positions was occurring at the same time the athletes were expected to be working with each other to overcome the opposition from outside. The individual athletes' healthy sense of competitive zeal, which drove them to perform, had to be balanced with an understanding of the team goals. My job was to nurture this sometimes contradictory set of values. I always emphasised that one's personal aims need not be different from those of the team – what is good for the individual can also be good for the team. Let's look at how this works in practice.

> **It is challenging and difficult to be a good team; you have to work at it.**

Individual responsibility leads to good team outcomes

There are many aspects of team functioning that need to be reconciled. Individuals are necessarily absorbed in their own performance so it is crucial that the link between individual performance and outcome for the team be underlined. In sport, too often the goal scorer or exceptional individual performer gets all the praise. Coaches must find ways to break down this traditional and simplistic analysis. Business leaders must also do this, emphasising the whole picture, not just the 'sexy' bits.

Nobody scored a goal against our team without us making a number of consecutive errors, usually four or five. A ball mishandled, someone out of position, an error in tackling, a

---

One's personal aims need not be different from those of the team.

---

mistake in reading the play, a missed interception or lazy chase, and then sometimes a goalkeeping slip-up. Often a brilliant piece of goalkeeping will prevent the goal, but too often the goalkeeper's miss is seized upon by observers as the error that cost the goal. However, it is the chain of consecutive mistakes that costs you. Similarly, to score we usually required a number of consecutive pieces of quality play. Clearly, taking the final shot requires skill and coolness, yet each piece of lead-up play brought about the scoring chance.

Thus we require individual thoroughness and single-incident determination in every piece of play. The athletes must understand that every one of these efforts adds cumulatively to the outcome of the match – the outcome for the team. Coaches should try hard to recognise and reward these individual efforts and establish an environment in which the athletes understand the connections to the outcome. This reinforces the creation of quality habits and thoroughness.

The analogy with business is strong. Winning a customer or a contract is usually the result of a number of inputs from different employees. It is seldom the result of a single masterstroke or effort. Great teams don't have a couple of special players or a special midfield, attack or defence. They have strength in every area, and that gives them resilience. Great individuals can be cut out or countered but great teams can only be overcome by an even greater team with strength in every area.

Within this context there is, of course, room for variety and individual brilliance and creativity. I always believed the team's tactics and way of

> **Winning a customer or a contract is usually the result of a number of inputs from different employees.
> It is seldom the result of a single masterstroke or effort.**

operating should take into account the various skills of its members. Coaches who try to confine the team members to a style of play that doesn't allow individual expression lose the essential strengths of many of the individuals. If, for instance, your organisation is strong in marketing but poor in customer service you should utilise your marketing strength while building up a customer service base. Be wary of trying to make good marketers into customer service people as you can lose out twice while not utilising your strengths.

Co-operation and co-ordination

How do you go about ensuring that your organisation is replete with individual endeavours that are co-operative and co-ordinated to get the outcome you seek? Co-ordination is merely a matter of scheduling. Co-operation is the difficult bit, for it involves a judgment to be made by the individual about the right thing to do in each situation. In sport, it requires split-second decision-making. This is developed by training, reviewing performances, rewarding and redirecting appropriately. The coach plays a role, as do fellow players. Over time you develop a culture of individual responsibility that underpins each individual involvement.

Usually we learn by experiencing what didn't work, which action wasn't right for the particular situation, which response brought the team grief. Our values underpin the correct actions – never expect something for nothing, share the load, work hard, never give in.

Similarly the values of your organisation can ensure co-operation. Management and employees reinforcing and using such a value framework in

---

Our values underpin the correct actions – never expect something for nothing, share the load, work hard, never give in.

---

your business will ensure co-operative actions and outcomes.

Co-operation has a moral element to it as it entails doing the right thing at the right time. Fortunately, moral actions are often an automatic response to the needs of others. Many people react positively when others are in danger or distress. They spontaneously do the right thing by virtue of their decency and sense of fair play. Managers and coaches must not let these impulses be lost in the cut and thrust of competition for they can embellish the co-operation of the group by reinforcing team values.

In teams, the goal of team achievement is enhanced when team members act to assist one another in such cases. In business, too, teamwork implies helping out, fixing problems and overcoming difficult situations that threaten our shared goals. While coaches and managers can instruct players and employees to do what is appropriate in the cauldron of competition, the individual's inclinations play an important part in determining the right actions. (This is another reason why quality selection is vitally important.) Co-operation – a willingness to help team-mates, to play a part, to do the right thing – is essential.

Sharing the load

Only by sharing the load, sharing all responsibility and sharing the rewards can teams work best. The nature of player contracts and the way they are negotiated in professional sport makes the coach's job much more difficult. Equally the ridiculous salaries sometimes paid to top management make the task of developing teamwork in an organisation very difficult. The strength of a team lies within the capacity of its individuals, and without their co-operation in each part of their business efficiency is diminished.

Co-operation is fostered by a sense of shared goals and shared rewards. I find it extraordinary that teams expect co-operation if the system of rewarding team members isn't equitable or related to performance. I believe that every organisation should aim to have share ownership by its employees, so they can all reap the rewards of success or suffer the consequences of failure.

In early 2000, the Hockeyroos voted to share any monetary rewards they might receive amongst the whole squad of twenty-five players, rather than only those who would play in the Sydney Olympics. When they made the decision, on their own, I was reassured that the team members were in the right place emotionally to share the burden of Olympic favouritism and the load of Olympic competition.

> **The strength of a team lies within the capacity of its individuals, and without their co-operation in each part of their business efficiency is diminished.**

A player on the field will often notice an opponent's state of fatigue or frustration or injury much better than a coach removed from the action. Similarly they will advise on the talk, fine detail and specifics of an individual's actions which the coach in the grandstand misses.

Two heads are better than one, six are better still

Coaches learn a great deal from their players, and in an important way the players are the coach's eyes and ears on the field. Their perspective is unique because they are in the heat of competition, and their opinions, ideas and suggestions provide crucial feedback for a coach. Ditto the employees in any organisation. Always listen to what your players or employees have to say – you may be surprised by what you learn.

Within the coaching team at the Hockeyroos we had some who were generalists and some with specific skills, for example, in psychology and physiology. Strategy, content, direction and methods were constantly reviewed and refined. I strongly believe six heads are better than one and the input of all the stakeholders improves the quality of your program or organisation.

Players, coaches, specialists and outside experts can all contribute to the mix of ideas and the flow of decision-making. By using a variety of resources you can draw on experience and knowledge that may be completely foreign to you. In the Hockeyroos, resourcing information from other sports and other countries enabled us to broaden our perspectives. Those who shun lateral input may be overly sure of themselves or afraid to experiment. Such an attitude is rarely useful. Indeed, if we expect the team to work co-operatively on the field, the off-field team

> **Good preparation and awareness of contingencies assist in the co-operative process.**

(the coaches) should display the same co-operative approach.

Of course at half-time or during a break in making a business presentation, there is not sufficient time for long consultations and coaches and managers must use their judgment to adjust tactics and strategy. The best prepared teams and workforces have already considered the possibilities and can implement previously identified responses. Good preparation and awareness of contingencies assist in the co-operative process.

Showing trust

One of the most difficult things for coaches to do is to let their team play. Once the game begins, in most sports, the coach only has a small input into what happens. Perhaps 5 per cent, maybe a little more. Once prepared, the athletes have to perform in the complex competitive environment of competition.

One of the best things I did in my coaching career was to play everyone. I decided very early on that I would not play with a bench. Every player would share the game time. Initially, I did this so that I could find out what all the players could do, but I soon discovered that given the opportunity many players exceeded my expectations – and surprised themselves as well.

Showing trust lifted their self-esteem, increased their sense of belonging and required them to perform. On the bench there is always an excuse. The sense of having to rely on each other and all being important and involved was a significant part of our sense of team.

> **Managers who allow their employees to review, report and restructure their own areas of responsibility show trust.**

Equally, the sharing of the coaching role was important to confirm that I practised what I preached. All members of the coaching staff had autonomy within their areas of responsibility. Teamwork must go throughout the team, on and off the field. Managers who allow their employees to review, report and restructure their own areas of responsibility show trust. In 2000 I asked the players to design our weekly training program for Sydney. I had to modify it because they made it too hard for themselves!

Some tips on building teamwork

1 Reward all who contribute to success. Acknowledgement, even with a trivial prize, can go a long way towards establishing belonging.

2 Make sure the 'chain of events' scenario is understood. Taking responsibility for single incidents underpins teamwork.

3 Openly discuss and establish a set of ethical values for the group.

4 Openly discuss team dynamics and the things that can cement the team together or pull the team apart. Selection stresses, poor results, poor form, injury, differential pay structures and personal disagreements can diminish co-operation and teamwork. Team members need to understand when and how these problems manifest themselves and be alert to deal with them.

5 Do role-playing exercises in which roles are reversed so people can understand and empathise with each other. Ask a player to be the coach who must inform a player they have been dropped or get an employee to act as manager and discipline a co-worker for a misdemeanour.

6 Ask team members to write down (anonymously) something they like about their fellow team members. Give each member a copy of all the things people liked about them. Once the group is more mature and resilient you might do the same thing with dislikes. In that case you might not give individual feedback but rather consider general issues that concern the group. (Note: team members receive only the input on themselves, not on others in the group.)

7 Show team members that you mean business and they are trusted. Play everyone in your team. Give everyone in your organisation opportunities. If you don't want to use them then don't select them!

8 Make sure that management shares the load and is seen to work co-operatively as part of the team. This does not mean there will not be some tension at times. This is normal in any dynamic organisation. Discussion of these tensions and how they manifest themselves is always valuable.

9 Work out ways to reward performances and efforts fairly – to share the benefits as well as the burden amongst everyone. Money is never a good enough reason to divide a team.

3 Learning and Training

I am often asked what quality best defined the Hockeyroos. What aspect of their approach was perhaps most pertinent to them being the world's best at what they did? My response usually surprises those listening for I believe it was the Hockeyroo's humility that was the defining characteristic of the group.

Humility

Humility does not imply shyness or lack of belief in what can be achieved. It does not suggest a lack of ambition. It is a state of being objective about yourself and your performance and is entirely consistent with being optimistic and determined about the future. It provides a good platform for learning and development. I doubt that any organisation that aspires to be excellent and wishes to sustain its performance does itself any good by vainglorious pronouncements or self-promotion. Such activities are distracting and unnecessary. In my experience, quality performance promotes itself sufficiently.

In the Hockeyroos, humility underpinned a belief that while successes tended to be transient, real excellence required us to improve and learn more. Nobody in the team had a perfect game. We could all add skills to our repertoire. We could all be mentally stronger and more resilient. We could all learn to make better decisions while under pressure.

Training is the rehearsal for performance

Sport captures our attention in a unique way. It is a drama in which performers and spectators do not know what will happen next. The performers in a TV show, play or movie must know their lines and cues in order for their timing to be right and the story to hold together. Modern movies take months, sometimes years, to be produced. Weeks of rehearsals go into any drama we view at the theatre. Athletes in competition must ad lib and their training sessions are the rehearsal for that performance.

Some sporting performances are similar to the rehearsal. The gymnast rehearses by repeating their routine until it is ready to be judged on the day of competition. The rehearsal helps perfect the execution and timing of the performance. Even in a sport such as swimming in which participants compete in races, the requirement is for perfect repetitious execution. While opponents can be seen and must be contended with, they are separated by lane ropes.

Team sports, however, such as football, basketball and hockey are much more complex and require the integration and co-operation of team members in a chaotic environment. Athletes in these complex integrated team activities are required to produce skills under the pressure of time, and in the face of hostile opponents.

In a way team sport mimics the environment of most businesses. The team members have to make decisions and judgments about what to do next throughout the match. In the end the sum total of those decisions and actions will determine the outcome. In the same way the sum total of decisions made and actions taken and the quality of those decisions and actions will determine how well a business performs. In business, where there is direct customer interaction at many different sites and at many different levels, the environment can be extremely chaotic, just as on the sporting field.

Most who watch sport regard the coach as the manager of the performance. Indeed the term 'manager' is used to describe the coaching role in many sports. While coaches and managers play a central role in determining strategy and tactics in any match or season, I believe nothing is more important than their role as teachers or trainers of their athletes. Once the game begins there is only a limited number of things that the coach on the sideline can do to affect the result. It is the athletes on the pitch or workers in the workplace who have to make the right play, make the correct decisions and be able to perform their skills under pressure.

Training produces excellent habits

Aristotle speculated about excellence: 'We are what we continually do; excellence is not an act, it is a habit.' He referred to skills and virtues as things we do by habit. Skills were measured by the product. A skilled craftsman produces fine works just as skilled athletes can flawlessly execute their craft. Perhaps more interesting was the moral dimension of Aristotle's view of virtue. He described virtues as habitual dispositions that involved choice and were moderated by reason.

In the same way that coaches train athletes to perform perfectly executed skills, they must also train athletes to make choices about what is the right thing to do in every situation. The execution of the right skill has to link with the actions and skills of team-mates. Accordingly skills cannot be learned only in isolation. They must be put in the context of team-mates, opponents and the game environment. The best athletes and workers are keen to learn more about themselves, their sport or work, its nuances, their team-mates and their opponents.

> **'We are what we continually do; excellence is not an act, it is a habit.'**

We learn best at work

Most students enter school, college or university believing their education at the institution is an end in itself. They think that once they have a diploma or degree, they will go out and get a job and begin a working life. Their learning days will be over. This perspective is completely wrong. Our school and university days only *prepare* us for the most important learning environment – the workplace. Once in the workplace, we must deal practically with the problems about which we have some theoretical knowledge.

Athletes who think that getting selected in

The best athletes and workers are keen to learn more about themselves, their sport or work, its nuances, their team-mates and their opponents.

---

the squad or team is the goal also miss the point. Even national team selection – the highest achievement – is only the beginning for those who aspire to be the best.

Training should be harder than the game, physically and mentally

The best training simulates the pressures and stresses of competition as well as providing the appropriate opportunity for skill acquisition that, initially, occurs best without the intensity of a competitive environment. For a national team, once a certain quality and competence is assumed, the training environment that is best is the one that reflects the reality of competition. Accordingly, my mantra for training with the Hockeyroos was that we had to make training physically and mentally more difficult than the game.

Most of us go through our lives without ever exploring our capacities, be they physical or mental. Most of us exercise until we are tired and stop. Elite athletes find they can push far beyond tiredness towards exhaustion. In order to improve fitness and strength physiologists understand the need to overload the body to get physical adaptation. Training for the Hockeyroos always included graded, planned overload to ensure improvement. In the same way we overloaded training with decisions and complexity in order to develop athletes who could handle a lot of information in an environment of hot competition and fatigue.

So athletes in our squad were training and learning in their workplace – in the international games, as well as going to 'school' when we were not playing in competitions. Additionally, they attended lectures and interactive sessions with coaches and other

Most of us go through our lives without ever exploring our capacities, be they physical or mental.

specialists and were expected to do their own investigative 'homework'. They were also learning about how to work co-operatively as a team in a practical everyday way, as well as theoretically in their many group sessions with our sports psychologist.

The environment created wasn't one of working at the job with a few bits of outside input as occurs in most businesses. It was full-on individual and team coaching, which integrated the practical and theoretical with physical, mental, tactical, technical and emotional development.

Training situations that entail situations where there are three competitors rather than two, or where you are working with reduced staff numbers would create a more complex and difficult environment. Asking people to work outside their present areas of competence could also work. Reversing the manager/staff roles helps create a far better empathy for one another as well as making 'training' harder.

Keep lifting the bar

Usually one learns most when one risks failing, when one risks going beyond what is comfortable. For athletes to learn optimally, the coach should challenge them to extend themselves, and the athletes should accept these challenges. Such an environment provides for growth and learning which can be very rapid. One of the secrets of extending an athlete's career is being able to challenge the athlete with appropriate tasks.

Perhaps most important is the self-discovery that can come from challenges of training and competition. The best athletes become able to monitor and chart their progress and development. Soon they start to ask the coaches

---

Usually one learns most when one risks failing, when one risks going beyond what is comfortable.

---

challenging questions. They provide feedback and a two-way communication ensues. Then you have an ideal learning situation for the exchanges and challenges are two-way, and the bar can be raised regularly. Once management and staff are communicating about performance and how to improve it they should be able to agree about new targets and new goals which represent progress. The challenge to improve stimulates investigation, analysis, evaluation and innovation.

This management style is particularly absorbing and requires confidence and very good communication. However, the rewards for employees, managers and businesses can be substantial.

> **The challenge to improve stimulates investigation, analysis, evaluation and innovation.**

Some tips for learning and training

1 Training situations should be designed to be more difficult than the normal job situation, that is, physically and mentally more taxing. (This might entail making the tasks complex and reducing the number of staff for the training exercise.)

2 Do role-playing exercises where ordinary staff act as the manager and vice versa. In such roles they should counsel an employee, sack someone, handle difficult clients and design company strategies. Managers assuming the role of an employee would also provide useful insight into the 'employee perspective'. Such experiences are always useful.

3 Encourage employees to question directives and make suggestions about how things can be improved. Employees' feedback is crucial to solidifying the relationship of management with staff.

4 Evaluate programs and share the information

obtained throughout the organisation. Ensure that this information is disseminated throughout the whole organisation.

5 Always ask why things were done and always be willing to explain why you did things a certain way. Six good questions to ask are: how, why, who, what, where and when.

6 Use a variety of methods to explain what you want done – illustrate with diagrams, use video replays, watch live performances, demonstrate and do, and get to know what works best in each situation.

7 Always make training interesting and fun. Nobody learns much when training becomes a chore rather than a passion. Little competitions, rewards and fun diversions can keep it fresh.

8 Watch others who are good in their field – other sports, other businesses and organisations.

9 Read widely and encourage the search for new ways to solve old problems.

4 Resilience

Something that is resilient will spring back into shape after it has been bent or distorted by some outside force. It has properties that give it the capacity to resume its starting form. In sport, resilience in the athletes and teams is a crucial quality to ensure reliable and consistent high performances.

Any task that is challenging and worth completing will not be finished without some disappointments. There will be obstacles along the way. In sport those disappointments can take many forms – non-selection, injury, poor form, a team loss or poor performance, group dis-harmony, personal distress in family or friends, funding cuts to the program – the list is long indeed. In business, you might face the obstacles of staff losses, new competition, opponents developing better products, collapse of suppliers, a changed business environment, increases in interest rates, etc., etc.

An often-repeated principle of coaching is to make things simple. This, of course, is what the greatest athletes are able to demonstrate with their timing, judgment, technique and physical gifts. Unfortunately, too many people confuse 'simple' with 'easy' – the very best can make things look simple because of their competence, but we should remember that many hours of

> **Too many people confuse 'simple' with 'easy' – the very best can make things look simple because of their competence, but we should remember that many hours of practice lie behind the simplicity.**

practice lie behind the simplicity. It has not been easily achieved, although it may indicate an ability in the athlete to focus on the important or priority areas, avoiding complication or distraction.

Every day human beings display their capacity to overcome distress, adversity, disability and failure. We often learn best from our mistakes and misadventures for those experiences sharpen our resolve to prepare better, know ourselves better, improve and learn. As Shakespeare, an acute and perceptive observer of the human condition, wrote in *As You Like It*, 'Sweet are the uses of adversity'. As we aim for our goals in life, we will invariably meet times when all seems lost or the chance appears impossible or out of our reach or outside our competence.

Mistakes are our friends

To the really resilient learner, mistakes are friends, not foes. Mistakes can make us stronger and more determined, or they can leave us disillusioned and defeated. My contention is that the only real defeat is death for it ends our capacity to adapt and change and improve. Of course, for athletes, time is something that takes away the capacity to physically compete, but it usually does not dull the ability to make judgments and act in most areas of life.

Each of us has a natural resilience. As I have already indicated, one only needs to observe the vagaries of life throughout the world to see examples of the most extraordinary resilience amongst humans of every colour, creed and circumstance. Those of us in the industrialised western nations think that life is tough if we dent the car, the share prices fall or we find a fly in our soup. We cannot even get close to imagining the stress felt by a mother who cannot find sufficient

> **Mistakes can make us stronger and more determined, or they can leave us disillusioned and defeated.**

food for her child or by those who live in lands beset by wars and conflicts. The viciousness of life under some totalitarian regimes probably never crosses our consciousness. Yet people everywhere cope with distress and display resilience. It is within all of us to do so.

One of the very good things about competition in sport is that it teaches us about success and failure in a non-hostile environment. In Kipling's words we should learn to 'treat these two impostors just the same'. Clearly, the capacity to put things in perspective and move on is crucial to our life instinct. We often lose control of our emotions during sporting performances and in moments of crisis at work, but we should remember that an ability to objectively analyse will go a long way to building resilience.

> **The capacity to put things in perspective and move on is crucial to our life instinct.**

Nothing is surer in life than the fact that things will go wrong, so we had better be prepared for it. Indeed part of being resilient is having a sober handle on what the possibilities are. In 1979, I remember walking disappointed from the hockey field after Australia lost to Pakistan 4–2 in the final of a ten-nation tournament in Perth. Asked by a journalist whether I had expected to lose, my response was, 'No, I never expect to lose any game, but I understand that it is always a possibility.' My answer, I think, was a realistic appraisal in a moment of stress.

Support, not dictation

Sporting contests require participants to solve problems and make decisions under extreme

> **I never expect to lose any game, but I understand that it is always a possibility.**

pressure in a cauldron of intense competition. Many of the responses are trained and instinctive. They are honed by intense practice and training – they are responses to the actions of others or initiated by one's capacity to sum up the situation and act decisively. In many interactions in business, the same sort of capacity is required and desirable. In interactions between customers and service providers, there are any number of situations which require the correct response at the point of contact.

Just as an athlete cannot step off the field to consult with the coach, and often cannot even refer to other players in the heat of competition, so also it is desirable for employees to have the training to handle every situation. But what if the last few times things went wrong or didn't work out? This is where resilience is crucial. Can we individually absorb the errors and mistakes and keep functioning next time? Can we learn and bounce back or do we lose confidence and trust in our ability to do it right next time?

Athletes, if they are in a positive learning mode, will accept criticism and redirection from their coach and act on it. They will be able to analyse what went wrong with the team and work at rectifying it. They will return stronger and more determined after defeat or injury or non-selection. The role of the coach is to encourage such behaviours and attitudes. The same is true of employees in any business. So how do you go about this?

Sometimes when things go wrong we find it difficult to handle. We can become depressed and negative. This is when objectivity and an ability to look at what really happened is important. The ability to identify the problems and provide solutions gives us a way forward, a reason to continue and hope for better. Our

Can we learn and bounce back or do we lose confidence and trust in our ability to do it right next time?

disappointment can often be a catalyst for such an approach or it can leave us wallowing in self-pity. Athletes, teams and organisations need to have the capacity to initiate such responses not only in the longer term but also in the moment.

Hard times endured and overcome together and recovery from disappointments and failures build our belief that 'it can be done'. Such experiences increase our faith in our ability to overcome setbacks and give us the will and the wit to fight back when things go wrong.

Managers and coaches have a crucial role in providing support and direction to their teams in times of crisis or disappointment. A focus on process, assistance with analysis and rectification, and optimism born out of experience are all

> **The ability to identify the problems and provide solutions gives us a way forward, a reason to continue and hope for better.**

useful inputs which can build resilience in the group. Dictating what should happen denies this crucial learning experience.

Let's now look at a real life story of resilience. Hockeyroo Jenny Morris displayed many exceptional qualities to become a dual Olympic gold medallist, but the most striking one was resilience.

Jenny Morris's story

Jenny Morris completed her undergraduate degree in psychology and communications at the end of 2001. She is now employed by a public relations firm in Perth. At thirty, in terms of academic achievement, career prospects and promotion she is way behind those she went to school with in Maryborough, central Queensland, or even those she started university with in Brisbane at the beginning of 1990.

In another respect, Jenny Morris is special. She has twice stood at the top of the podium on the closing days of two Olympic Games. She is a double Olympic gold medallist.

In 1991, Jenny Morris suffered an anterior cruciate ligament tear and had her right knee reconstructed. She worked hard to recover and went close to selection for the Barcelona Olympics. Perhaps she would have made that team in 1992 if not for her knee problem. Five years later, when her playing ability was in its prime, Jenny suffered another severe blow. Playing in a finals match in Perth in September 1997, Jenny suffered a similar injury to her left knee. This time recovery was slower and more difficult. In 1998 and 1999 Jenny made only a few appearances for Australia and endured much frustration and disappointment.

Throughout 1998 Jenny worked hard to rebuild her leg. The muscles were wasted, and for function to fully return Jenny had to undertake stringent workouts twice daily. She was not ready to play in the 1998 World Cup in June, nor in the Commonwealth Games in Kuala Lumpur.

Late in 1998 she travelled with the Hockeyroos to Buenos Aires for her first hockey of the year. She performed fairly, but was troubled by continuing unexplained pain and additionally had developed patello-femoral pain under her kneecap. As 1999 dawned the future was still unclear, but as the months passed it became apparent that further surgical intervention and an extended period of rehabilitation would be required. Jenny missed the Champions Trophy in June and another season had passed without her re-establishing her place in the team. For athletes, injury, poor form or non-selection can be devastating, but in my experience nothing is more debilitating and demotivating than a long-term injury.

Resilience is the ability to handle setbacks – to see your way through them, to persist in the face of doubt and uncertainty. There were many times when Jenny felt she would not make it back into the team. That she did was a great credit to her. Our program provided support;

Jenny remained a squad member and was sustained by her scholarship and the friendship of team-mates. On a number of occasions Jenny and I sat down together to discuss progress and her prognosis. More than once the sessions ended in tears without a satisfactory outcome. Jenny wanted to play, and I wanted her to play but it would have been counterproductive to do so too soon as her recovery had become complicated. Jenny was willing to push harder, but 'more' was not necessarily 'better' and in her case, recovery required real patience and resolve. Holding her back was difficult at times.

By early 2000, Jenny Morris was ready to play, and week by week she asserted herself more and more until it became clear that she would again be a significant force in the Hockeyroos. There were disappointments along the way. At times it appeared she had lost much of her former mobility and skill, but these occasions became less frequent and less pronounced. Jenny's persistence and resilience paid off as in

August 2000 she was selected in the team to play in the Olympics. But even in the last days before the Games began a muscle strain threatened her position. She overcame that final hurdle and her second-half goal in the Olympic final was recognition that she had completed her journey.

Jenny always knew she was wanted and that we believed she could do it. She lost three of her most productive sporting years, but I am sure when she looks back on her time it will seem worth it.

Many athletes might not have made it to Sydney. Jenny admits she went close to giving up a few times but she stuck at it and kept going at those difficult times. I like to think I helped her stay positive and showed faith in her. I think her team-mates provided great support as did those who helped her rehabilitate. More than anything perhaps having been through it before also helped her. In the end it probably was an amalgam of all these things that kept her going.

Some tips on building resilience

1 Make sure everyone understands the **why** of what you are doing. For example, you could say, we must train this hard in order to obtain the necessary fitness...it is not because I'm a sadist! Or, we lost because we did not do certain things well...we can improve by correcting those errors and this is how we can do it.

2 Be realistic about success and failure, always look behind the outcome and have a process orientation. The outcome looks after itself once you get the processes right.

3 Set realistic goals and be aware of the problems that possibly will be faced.

4 Never be afraid to lose. Encourage enterprise. Too many teams are afraid to take risks and accordingly play very conservatively. You must risk losing to win and learn to take calculated risks.

5 Make the training intense and harder than real work or the game. That way you build resilience in the least threatening environment first.

6 Provide criticism and redirection in a way that encourages and provides answers to the problems identified. Criticism should always be couched in a way that also identifies strengths and positive solutions.

7 Encourage ownership of the organisation. In business that might mean allocating or encouraging share ownership among employees. In sport it means the athletes should be given direct access to the program and its planning, direction and content. This increases the team's belief that they can fix things, together with the coaching staff, when they go wrong or don't work out as anticipated.

5 Building Depth and Flexibility

You often see teams do well and then appear reluctant to change much or to introduce new players or methods. Companies are also often guilty of this 'fortress mentality'. Those who may have strived hard for success believe they earned it and want to hold on to it for themselves. Equally, they may have a few very competent people in their team and the loss of a couple of them might undermine the whole capacity of the organisation to perform.

Depth and flexibility are essential in any enterprise that aims to be successful. In both the sporting and work context achieving depth and flexibililty entails multiskilling, so that your organisation has the capacity to keep performing if circumstances change. Depth and flexibility are crucial if we wish to handle change successfully, adapt to change, accept change and keep on track with our core activity.

Expect change and anticipate change

In sport, changes occur for many reasons: injury or illness, poor form, opposition tactics and strengths, the retirement of aging players, new rules. There are many reasons why flexibility is crucial. In 1993 when I first began with the Hockeyroos, I believed we had a number of very good midfielders and so we developed a way of playing that enabled us to utilise all of those players. However, defence and attack could not be ignored. Indeed, those were the areas where we could capitalise on our midfield superiority.

It was important that our midfielders had the capacity to score when in attack and defend our goal when required. In order to ensure that this was the case, the midfielders were encouraged to acquire and practise the skills used by the attackers and defenders. Equally, the attackers and defenders needed more than just the craft associated with their particular designation. We could lose players suddenly through illness or injury – we had to expect that – but because we anticipated that change, we always had other players ready to take over. In business, if you do not have strategies for dealing with staff changes you will struggle when this situation arises. Multiskilling workers provides some of the best coverage for such events.

Prepare for change

There were many occasions over the eight years I was with the Hockeyroos when we had injuries or unavailable players. I was always confident that we could overcome our opponents in such situations because I knew our players were capable of holding down a number of positions if required. Indeed, in team selection, we always ensured that we had a few options for every position. The best preparation for sudden changes is to practise adapting to change. We did this by requiring players to play unfamiliar positions in training and in games, and by emphasising the need to multiskill every player.

By insisting on flexibility, we had coverage and some depth. We also built depth by introducing new players and providing opportunity for some on the periphery to play. We were 'inclusive' rather than 'exclusive', and opened up our squad to a range of players who were considered to be on the margins of the team. This

> **The best preparation for sudden changes is to practise adapting to change.**

was a conscious process aimed at expanding the number of players with international experience and providing opportunities for them to display their wares.

During my stint as coach, fifty-four players played for the Hockeyroos, yet only twenty-seven (half of them) played in the main competitions. For everyone who played in the Olympics or World Cups, there was a player who was given opportunity but didn't make the final selection for the major competitions. All of those twenty-seven were given opportunities and played international games for their country.

Be inclusive

I sometimes tell the story of Danni Roche, who had been in the Australian squad for a couple of seasons, travelled overseas and played only a few minutes in a couple of years. Reintroduced into the squad in 1994, she played herself into the Olympic team in 1996 and her last game for

Australia was the Olympic final in Atlanta. She is a gold medallist now. Without being given a further chance to show what she could do, she may never have played for Australia again.

Some of those who are given opportunity don't make the grade, but hopefully they leave the game knowing that they did their best and were given every chance to show their wares. They will be content knowing that they gave it their best shot. They need not live their lives wondering 'What if?'. I believe it is only by being inclusive in our approach and by providing real opportunities that we build depth in our organisation.

Often when the Hockeyroo coaches discussed the team we differed in our assessments. Who was the best? Who would make it? Who would improve? The practical tests of performance in competition usually gave us answers to these questions, and as athletes spent time in our program our judgments and assessments were refined.

As a general principle we always had at least three or four options for every position in our squad and were aware of those outside the squad who could be considered 'next in line', as well as those who were developing in our junior squads. In this way, whatever the circumstances, whichever team we chose could perform. Every business should have people who can do one another's jobs, and I believe it is worth formally assessing and assigning who those people will be. It should not create tension if done sympathetically. It will provide for a better understanding of how the whole team or organisation holds together and what each person contributes.

Of the 253 matches that we played during my tenure as coach, only thirty (11.9 per cent) were in major tournaments. Those games were highly competitive. Many of our other games

> **Every business should have people who can do one another's jobs.**

were used for polishing our team. In those matches building depth in our squad was one of our principal aims. The best coaches are able to identify talent and mostly get it right, but there were many occasions when I underestimated a player's ability or rate of improvement, or some aspect of their game. So I was often pleased that we chose an inclusive approach rather than narrowly focusing on the perceived 'best' talent available.

Don't forget succession

My experience in coaching, politics and from observing business is that managers often surround themselves with 'like-minded' souls who are supportive but often too agreeable and seldom challenging. Really smart bosses never appoint 'yes men' and don't fear challenging and ambitious staff members. Such people provide creativity and vibrance to the organisation. They know the organisation well and throw up ideas about how it can be improved. They readily supply the drive to ensure succession as well as making the work environment creative. They promote flexible thinking.

The organisation or team needs to retain its knowledge and learn from its history. Staff and coaches, just like athletes, need ongoing updating and training. Rather than lose experience, the best teams and organisations will continually throw up prospective leaders and managers from within. Ambitious people aren't a threat to the bosses unless they are too impatient. (This characteristic would rule them out of contention anyway.)

Hockeyroo Claire Mitchell-Taverner is someone whose story emphasises the value of depth, flexibility and multiskilling.

Claire Mitchell-Taverner's story

In 1993, I noticed Claire Mitchell-Taverner, a slightly built but skilful and neat striker from Victoria. While her skills were good, she was without the dynamism and strength that is often needed by strikers to operate in close quarters. She was not really quick but appeared to have a good head for the game in that she could find space. However, something about her said that she wasn't quite right to be a striker in our team.

Enquiries revealed that Claire had been in the Australian team previously and in the Australian Institute of Sport squad in 1990. At the end of the year she was released from the squad and returned home to Melbourne without making an Australian team. At the end of 1993, we resurrected her career when we took her to Europe as a reserve to play a couple of matches before the Champions Trophy tournament started, as our captain, Rechelle Hawkes, was recovering from an injury. During the next couple of years we discovered that Claire had a very good aerobic capacity. With her penchant for scoring, we thought that she might be suited to playing as an attacking midfielder.

Indeed, during the time before Atlanta, Claire worked at making herself into a reliable midfielder. Her defensive orientation was still not sound (she had been a striker all her career) but by the time we got close to Atlanta, Claire was in the final wash-up for selection. In a close adjudication she just missed out. As a striker she would have been well off the pace; as an attacking midfielder she went very close to selection. Perhaps she did not have the defensive qualities required, perhaps she was still not a good enough passer and perhaps she still lacked the strength to impose herself on a game.

Crestfallen after missing Atlanta, Claire came close to retiring. However, we managed to persuade her to continue. She could still add things to her game and our investment in her had seen significant development. At twenty-six, her best years could be ahead of her. Claire worked at her game, and in the 1998 World Cup final she played one of her best-ever matches to help the team turn an early deficit, in front of a stadium full of parochial Dutch supporters, into a win against the home team.

By 2000, Claire was an integral part of our attacking midfield. She maintained her penchant for scoring, gleaned from her years as a striker in Victoria. However, her trapping, passing and endurance by then provided real body to our team. When I think about our gold-medal win in Sydney, the aspects I perhaps remember best are Claire's timely interventions in our defensive circle. These efforts saved us on more than one occasion, and at crucial times. Defence was never part of Claire's natural instinct for the game, but these defensive skills were learned as she strove to become multiskilled.

Until 1997, I was never sure that Claire would make it into our best team. However, I worked hard to convince her that she should continue in order to discover for herself just how far she could go. I never assured her of selection but always believed that our team was only as good as its peripheral players. As these players, who provided depth, improved and challenged the senior group, we had a dynamic that ensured the right type of internal competition. Two of Claire Mitchell-Taverner's best games for Australia were the final at the World Cup in 1998 and the gold-medal game at the Sydney Olympics. She was in many ways the best fulfilment of a policy of developing depth and flexibility. Every organisation should strive to do so.

Some tips for building depth and flexibility

1 Expect every player or employee to know the salient or central aspects of some other positions.

2 Require them to perform these roles and skills at training or theoretically through role-playing and discussion.

3 Test them in serious match or workplace situations and develop an environment of challenge and exploration.

4 Prepare for contingencies. Play with players missing or try different and experimental tactics.

5 Trawl the talent and include people about whom you may not be sure. Have maximum squad size because someone will always surprise you. Include some in your squad who may be down on skill but really want to learn and do their best. In your business give all employees training and opportunities. Some people who appear less qualified will surprise you.

6 Give flexibility teeth – present it as a selection strength.

7 Monitor changes in your business and be ready to respond to them. Never fear change for it is inevitable.

8 Enjoy change as it gives you a chance to express yourself in new and exciting ways.

9 Ignore youth at your peril. Young people play and work with freedom and exuberance and concentrate the minds of everyone else in the group. (More on this in chapter 8.)

PART 2

The Five Principles of Staying the Best

Once someone has achieved success – won the premiership or championship or gold medal, had a record-breaking year, seen massive profit growth, moved ahead of an opponent in the share market – the tendency is to relax and enjoy the experience, praise or high altitude. Unfortunately, this is especially the case when the goal was to 'succeed' – whatever that may have meant for the individual, team or company.

Those who have the capacity to stay at the top are driven by a different ethos. Their satisfaction and pleasure comes from doing things well. It comes from being in an environment that is stimulating, challenging and demanding, and it comes from their ability to lose themselves in the task. Often, it is the burden of expectation of others that can prove distracting. Equally, the praise and backslapping of an admiring public, media or supporters can derail the best outfits.

In this respect sporting achievement is often both unrealistic and much more demanding than business endeavours, or indeed the challenges of succeeding in everyday life because it can focus on one season, tournament or game rather than more sustained performances.

Those who aspire to a university degree and work throughout the year diligently will usually be successful and achieve their aim. Even a large percentage of those slacking in the course will do likewise. Yet at football there will be just one winner at the end of the year. Similarly, in our relationships or working lives it is very rare that our performance or ability will be tested on one day in such a way that we will succeed or fail. Usually, assessments are made over time, balancing all efforts to reach an outcome.

The secret of success in sport and in other

The secret of success in sport and in other endeavours is to not be distracted by the expectations and ambitions of others and to be able to stay on task.

---

endeavours is to not be distracted by the expectations and ambitions of others and to be able to stay on task. Those who best do that are invariably those who are able to enjoy the journey without becoming too focused on the outcome. Every one of us might know this, but usually along the way we lose sight of why we are doing something and what the important elements are. Accordingly, two of the keys to staying at the top are an ability to keep our eye on what it is that made us good in the first place, and the need for coaches and managers to **keep coaching** and take nothing for granted. There is a great

> **Two of the keys to staying at the top are an ability to keep our eye on what it is that made us good in the first place, and the need for coaches and managers to keep coaching and take nothing for granted.**

tendency for the coach or manager to leave the best players or workers to their own devices and to no longer monitor or evaluate their performance. Equally, there is often a resistance to advice amongst this group of athletes or workers. Neither of these things optimises performance. As a senior athlete, I felt I suffered from a lack of coaching when I wanted more input. Very often, by the time the coach or manager wakes up to this deficiency it is too late. I have no doubt that there were times at the end of my playing career when I needed more intervention and support in order to maximise my performance.

The other elements that are crucial once your organisation is at the top are for you to keep making the environment interesting and absorbing. You must **refresh the team**, **redefine the challenges**, **avoid recycling** and **face your foes**. The foes of your organisation are often part of the trappings of success. Silent enemies such as acceptance, doubt and expectation must be confronted and dealt with for you to continue to develop and grow.

The introduction of youth is perhaps the thing that best refreshes the group. For many who have already achieved much, the task of staying at the top is facilitated by redefining their challenges. Consistent with these two approaches is the desire to continue to innovate and enhance what is in place to avoid recycling.

The following chapters will look at each of the five principles of staying at the top in turn, though, as in Part 1, elements of each chapter will overlap. The principles are:

- Continue with the core principles and keep coaching
- Redefine the challenges
- Refresh the team
- Avoid recycling
- Face your foes.

6 Continue with the Core Principles and Keep Coaching

Most successful organisations and teams reach the stage where they forget what it was that made them great. You can see examples of this all the time in sport. Teams emerge and are built up, usually through getting together a group of quality players who complement each other and grow and learn together. Commonly, teams or organisations start to slip because in the minds of the athletes or staff those core values fall out of sight. Of course some teams have had periods where they have bucked this trend. Phil Jackson's Chicago Bulls, Vince Lombardi's Green Bay Packers, the West Indies cricket team of the 1980s and Alex Ferguson's present Manchester United team all come to mind. However, such sustained periods of quality are rare. Should the French World Cup-winning soccer team be able to retain the 2002 World Cup in Japan, they would also have claims.

How often do clubs retain their great players for a season or two too long? How often do they forget the need for youthful, energetic recruitment, once an established senior team is in place? How often are emotional decisions made about sticking with strategies that used to work? How often are players distracted by fame, money, media attention or sponsors' requests to the detriment of their performance? How often do the management or staff become comfortable with the trimmings of success and take their eye off the game and lose their previous passion to keep improving, learning, challenging and coaching?

The answer to every question is 'often'. Many people believe this is inevitable, and that the cycle of success is the norm. The challenge of staying at the top is to continue with the core principles and values and to keep coaching once you reach the top. Developing depth and flexibility is part of the story. Maintaining vigilance about all the things that can disrupt the organisation is another, and implementing plans for succession is essential.

With the Hockeyroos, we endeavoured to continually renew the group and were always aware of the future requirements of the team. This entailed building depth and flexibility by including a group of players continually being prepared for future roles in the team. Even with the retirement of eight or nine players after the Sydney Olympics, there was at least the same number with a couple of years of senior experience to take their place.

Of course, coaches do not usually choose their successors and organisations tend to look outside themselves for replacements. This makes sense if things are not right; however, in a successful program much good knowledge can be lost in a complete clean-out. I firmly believe that good organisations should train and prepare future management. This is an important part of building depth and flexibility. It was always interesting for the Hockeyroos to watch other countries change their coaches, searching for that special chemistry to bring success. Invariably, there was a different approach with the new coach – sometimes beneficial, sometimes not so – but there was always another period during which the new coach was a novice not really knowing the other teams as well as his or her predecessor! Over time, I believe, the accumu-

> **Good organisations should train and prepare future management.**

lated knowledge of our group was a significant advantage as it helped us counter other teams' strengths and exploit their weaknesses.

So once you have tasted success, do the core principles of being the best lose their relevance? The answer is an emphatic 'NO'.

Quality

Quality remains an imperative in recruitment and selection of personnel and in designing and implementing the processes of the organisation. The advantage of being at the top is that you should already have good knowledge of what it takes to be the best. Having made mistakes, you should be able to avoid the gaffes of the past. You should also be able to attract the best personnel.

Co-operation

Perhaps the element most essential for those wanting to stay at the top is continued co-operation and teamwork. Most teams suffer from what I call 'group disintegration' over time. The 'we' becomes 'me' and individuals tend to focus on their own issues over team issues. Coaches and managers must realise that co-operation is not a static thing. The interactions between team members require constant monitoring and management. Coaches should see this as a priority when success has been attained as those who would influence and distract players (media, sponsors, employers, managers, fans) grow in number and vociferousness.

This issue received constant attention in the Hockeyroos after the gold-medal win in Atlanta, and indeed our decision from 1999 to no longer have a captain was partly a reaction to stresses that can cause a group to disintegrate.

By requiring every member of the team to consider themselves as team leaders with responsibilities to the team, we hoped that we could get them to think outside themselves. Equally, we constantly tried to address the stresses and anxi-eties that cause groups to divide. Insight into how we are less tolerant when self-absorbed or distracted by outside influences is the first line of defence against such intolerance.

Training and learning

Over the period you are trying to build a quality program, you will find good ways to prepare. Once you have reached the top, training can easily become a little mundane, and after a while successful team members or staff members may start to think they know it all and have done it all before.

The coach has a responsibility to provide variety in training and to renovate the methods that helped the team make it to the top. While on the way up the athletes' focus on being the best may help them overlook worn-out methods; once the heights are scaled, the danger of things becoming passé is greatly increased.

Whether you coach the Under 10s in the local park or a national team, it is crucial that training sessions be interesting and fun. Equally, those who manage businesses have a responsibility to make training and the work environment places where people want to go. Staff must feel their time is spent in worthwhile ways and that they are making progress that can be measured.

Resilience

Resilience is usually an outcome of making it to the top. However, the seduction of the glamour and comfort of success can easily play a part in causing us to forget those experiences that build resilience. The coach or manager at the top must remind athletes or workers of those difficult experiences that forged individuals into a tough

> **It is crucial that training sessions be interesting and fun.**

resilient group. A fall from grace for some athletes or workers is often the best catalyst to renew their acquaintance with the hard times.

Once at the top, an organisation becomes a target for all opponents. A team or organisation in such a position is closely scrutinised and everyone wants to defeat it. Consequently, every team plays at their best against the top team – there are no easy games. Perhaps one of the things that most commonly occurs in sport is that teams underestimate opponents; I certainly believe such a mindset is the background to many upsets.

However, the top team gets no such luxury. They are never underestimated and indeed every underdog opponent pulls out all their best shots against them. I always said to our players that this was a great advantage for us because we never had an easy game. Any time we relaxed or

> **Once at the top, an organisation becomes a target for all opponents.**

were sloppy, teams were alert and ready to make us pay. I believe this made us tougher and accustomed us to playing under pressure and at high tempo. In the end, it would help us handle the stresses of major tournaments, for we would be used to pressure games.

Any business at the top of its game is similarly subjected to intensive competition. This competition is greatest when you are the industry standard. Used properly, it can make you more diligent, alert and resilient. It makes you even better.

Depth and flexibility

If you have paid attention to this part of your organisation's development, you will be in a good

> **Ensuring depth and flexibility is not something you should start to look at when you've made it!**

position to continue being successful. I believe it is lack of attention to this area on an ongoing basis that brings teams and organisations down.

Ensuring depth and flexibility is not something you should start to look at when you've made it! It is something that needs to be in place on the way up. This is true both of players and staff, and coaches and managers. Without having sufficient depth in the pipeline and a plan for succession you will falter, and without a focus on flexibility you will not be able to handle the inevitable crisis that will come along in every season or business cycle.

The critical rule here is to emphasise, plan for and implement depth and flexibility from the start. Keep doing it and don't stop when you reach the top.

Never make the mistake of thinking the senior staff or players don't require attention.

Don't forget your senior people

I have outlined how we must continue to push the core values or principles once we have achieved success. The success issues that helped you make it remain seminal to what you continue to do. It is also necessary to continue to coach *everyone*. Never make the mistake of thinking the senior staff or players don't require attention. While the new personnel are often keenly seeking knowledge, too often the senior people are forgotten. Keep coaching the senior players!

The five pillars of good coaching

It is worth reminding ourselves of the character-istics that coaches and managers need to con-stantly display and demonstrate if they are to be listened to and respected. These are my five pillars of coaching:

1 Have the **knowledge**, keep up to date and try to stay at the edge of discovery.

2 **Work harder** than anyone else. Always be prepared and be willing to stay as long as necessary. Have time for everyone.

3 **Listen** to everyone – make time for that and be willing to incorporate new ideas that warrant attention. Be flexible – sometimes at half-time or even 10 minutes into the game the strategy or game plan needs revision.

4 **Be consistent** in your interactions with the athletes or staff, whether rewarding, reprimanding or redirecting. There is always a way to be positive. Find it.

5 **Be honest** and direct about yourself and in your interactions. People can handle bad news or criticism if it is appropriately delivered and comes from someone they respect. It will then serve as a catalyst for improvement and growth.

7 Redefine the Challenges

If you are serious about staying at the top every coach or manager has to be constantly searching for new ways to test and extend themselves and those they are working with. Lisa Powell's story illustrates this point very well.

Lisa Powell's story

In the Barcelona Olympics in 1992, Lisa Powell was crestfallen when the team finished outside the semi-finals. One of the favoured teams leading into the competition, Australia finished fifth. Four years later in Atlanta, Lisa achieved her Olympic goal when she was part of Australia's midfield engine. She scored three goals and performed consistently, and at times brilliantly, through the tournament.

Lisa had achieved her lifelong ambition and indeed throughout 1996 had worked as hard as she could to be in peak physical condition. An early season hamstring injury that threatened her year had worried her, but she had been diligent and overcame it. Though anxious by nature, Lisa was also very competitive and determined. Yet she was often too tense for her own good. This manifested itself most in her goal shooting when the pressure to take a shot sometimes produced an anxious or rushed effort. Fortunately, she was very quick and agile, naturally well balanced and fluent, and she possessed good basics and very good passing, especially when assessing options at a distance or in the broad field of play.

As we moved into 1997, Lisa appeared a little

uncertain about what to do in hockey. She played serviceably and was still a good performer at club and state level, but I wondered whether she would be what we wanted for the Sydney Olympics. Certainly on her 1997 form the answer was no. The major competition in 1997 was the Champions Trophy in Berlin, which brought together the best six nations. Lisa was not included in the Hockeyroo team and although called to Germany as an emergency replacement in the days before the competition, she was not required and was sent back home when the competition started.

I believe it was in the month or so after that episode that Lisa's career was resurrected and given new definition and purpose. We won in Berlin but I was concerned that we didn't have enough pace in our defence, following the retirement from hockey of Nova Peris. I approached Lisa about the possibility of her playing as a defender. I believed the challenge of a new position, which would require her to learn new skills and totally rethink her approach to hockey, could regenerate her interest and enthusiasm. Lisa said that at the time she was considering whether she would continue. She was a bit lost and had just drifted into her old routine. She was not really enjoying her game.

Six weeks later we travelled to Seoul with a half-strength team to play Korea, Argentina, England, Canada and the Netherlands in the inaugural Telekom Cup. These teams represented four of the world's best six nations at the time. Lisa, one of only four senior players in the team, played at left half (for the first time, ever) throughout, and in that short period showed that she might be able to do the job. Lisa remembered the time well. She now says that the approach about playing in defence was 'the one comment that sparked me back to life again. It was exciting to consider the new challenge, it gave me something new to aim for. I found a reason to keep playing.'

A year later she was more than adequate in

defence at the World Cup, where one of her passes proved match winning, and by the time 2000 came around Lisa, in my view, was the best and most accomplished left-sided defender in the women's game. She improved her tackling and positioning, her pace was invaluable to our whole back line, and her passing and ability to penetrate and run the ball were the world's best. Lisa overcame much of her performance anxiety, as I believe her new role gave her the opportunity to openly face her anxiety demons. On top of all that she showed great courage and determination by frequently putting her body on the line. In her old position of midfielder, she would only occasionally have been tested in that way.

For me, as a coach, the example of Lisa Powell (now Lisa Carruthers) and her resurrection as a team member was the best example of what I believe is a critical principle of management. Of the nine players in the team in Sydney who had also played in Atlanta, only the goalkeeper, Clover Maitland, did not at some stage play in a new position. This was not just part of building depth and flexibility, it represented an active program of challenging and refreshing the team and individuals. More than half of that group found themselves with completely different roles in Sydney. All of the others were required to test themselves elsewhere and were challenged to be competent in a variety of different roles.

Lisa Carruthers, now retired with a baby and living in Sydney with husband Stuart, extended and embellished her career by being willing to redefine the challenges of her game.

Skills don't go but purpose can

In sport, the examples are many: Australian cricketer Justin Langer's rediscovery as an opening batsman; Justin Leppich moving from full forward to fullback for the Brisbane Bears, sprinters Raelene Boyle and Betty Cuthbert coming back to win over 400 metres. Very often the proven performer only requires something like the move to a new position to catalyse their endeavours, refocus their efforts, reignite their passion and get them actively working on their craft. Similarly, in the workplace it is often those who are comfortable and feel able to do their jobs without too much hassle who need to be challenged with new tasks, new demands and new requests.

New challenges help solve old problems

A new environment and new challenges often provide an opportunity to face issues that have

> **In the workplace it is often those who are comfortable and feel able to do their jobs without too much hassle who need to be challenged with new tasks, new demands and new requests.**

been avoided in another role. Lisa Powell was anxious about her new role, but given that no one expected her to be on top of it immediately, she became more open about seeking advice. Equally, while her anxious disposition didn't go away, the new role allowed her to seek assistance in managing that part of her demeanour. In the past as a 'competent senior player', she had appeared less keen to ask for help. Along with Lisa's discovery of her new mental, technical and tactical capacities came a new empathy for others in the team and her contribution to the whole tone of the team was terrific.

To lesser degrees, we found similar responses from others who were tested by new demands and grew in their new roles. While the challenge for the team was essentially the same as previously, the new individual aspirations and tasks allowed those who had done it before to go about doing it again but in a completely new way. Clearly, the capacity of managers, coaches and individuals to set themselves new challenges and to redefine old goals can be crucial to sustaining quality performance.

In their book *Peak Performance*, Clive Gilson, Mike Pratt, Kevin Roberts and Ed Weymes discuss the psychology of sustaining peak performance. They say 'challenges once met are no longer challenges . . . the challenge itself must be enriched or renewed periodically'. The French poet and philosopher Paul Valéry, in correspondence with André Gide, put it thus: '*Il faut se donner un but impossible*' – 'We must set ourselves an impossible goal.' Goals *must* challenge the best of our abilities and skills. When they force us to strike out into new territory, they expand our expectations of ourselves and give purpose and fascination to our endeavours.

In my book *The Coach* I referred to those who need new challenges as 'terminal players'. Every organisation, business or group has terminal players; those who think they know it all, are comfortable, may even be competent but are just going through the motions. Generally they have lost the excitement and enthusiasm that made them good, and once identified they are best moved on if they are unwilling to take on new challenges.

Some tips on how to redefine the challenges

1 As well as the players, management and coaches can change the paradigm with new roles, new skills and new relationships. Be wary of comfortable 'done it all before' types.

2 Make it clear that nobody is indispensable.

3 Get everyone to redefine their own job to improve it, and also to nominate the role or position they would most like if they were to change. Ask everyone what they think is the toughest job in the organisation. Then ask them how they would do it. In doing so they often discover their own new ambitions and have their ambitions extended.

4 New technology can change your challenges and requirements; don't be afraid of it, embrace it. In sport, changes to the rules can dramatically change the 'job description'; for example after 1996, the concept of 'being offside' was removed from hockey, thus causing a rethink about the methods and tasks entailed in many positions.

5 Question how things were done before – is there a better way or a better person? What can we add? What should we retain or improve?

6 Look outside your business or sport for examples of similar situations or challenges.

7 Experiment and take some risks, but make them calculated and don't neglect the core details.

8 Refresh the Team

Just as individuals need to be renewed and refreshed by new challenges, so does your team. The individuals can be given new roles and tasks yet the goals for the team also need to be renewed and refreshed. Nothing refreshes a team more than the introduction of new talent and new faces.

Ignore youth at your peril

Young talented players simultaneously threaten, inspire and awaken those who are too comfortable. They bring innocence and excitement and often possess skills different from those of established team members. They can help individuals and the group rediscover their passion and enthusiasm for the game. They are at once free of expectations yet while they may have doubts they seem less burdened by them than many senior players with whom they are competing. It seems they feel they have less to lose.

What they lack in finesse and subtlety, they make up in vibrancy, desire and willingness to learn and improve. They often play an important role in the rediscovery of these qualities by others in the team, and they remind everyone that nothing is certain or lasts forever.

Angie Skirving's story

In 1997, I first spied Angie Skirving, then a gangling sixteen-year-old, still raw but with the demeanour of a much older player. She was the best of the youngest group of players I thought might be ready to play in the senior team at the Sydney Olympics. You can never be sure how a young player will progress at the top level, but having seen Angie only once I thought we should ensure that between then and the Sydney Olympics there should be opportunity for her to develop and for us to measure her progress.

At the end of 1998, we took Angie overseas with our team to Argentina. In a team replete with young players, Angie was the youngest at seventeen. She acquitted herself satisfactorily and in 1999, after she had finished school, we brought her to Perth to be part of the Hockeyroos program. Angie struggled with the intensity and the workload and it was necessary to modify her program. Angie was homesick too, but she was slowly starting to see herself as a senior team player. When asked about that time now, she insists she usually felt that she could never be as good as the others. She worried she would not be asked back the next year, yet she also saw glimpses of form which led her to think she could make it.

In that year Angie was erratic in her performance. At times she trained and played with the best of them. At other times we were at a loss to know how to lift her out of lethargy and uncertainty. However, she had one crucial and unbending quality. She was very determined to succeed and by the year's end her selection in our squad of twenty-five for the Olympic year was not controversial. Angie felt she was lucky to be there – she knew she wanted to make the most of her opportunity.

At the beginning of 2000, each of the coaching staff picked what we thought would be our Olympic team for September. Only one of the three coaches selected Angie, but after the first few weeks of training all three of us had lifted our expectations of her. Angie had seemingly taken a quantum leap forward after the long break and was in the sort of form and frame of mind that said 'pick me'. Even then, Angie's recollection is of feeling she had improved but was still off the pace.

While during 1999 she had seemed erratic and uncertain at times, in February 2000 she was in control, stronger, improving at breathtaking pace and seemingly afraid of no one. While one or two of the others seemed apprehensive about selection, Angie, with little expectation, was just going for it. As the year progressed, Olympic selection seemed a possibility.

It was something I have seen so often in sport. The young tyro can play seemingly without fear or expectation and more senior players are plagued by doubts. It seems like it is the wrong way around. Of course, Angie was a gifted athlete: tall, fast, a great tackler and also brave. What happened to her in this period?

Recently, I asked Angie about that time. She told me that as the season progressed and she was selected for more matches, she started to think she could make the Olympic team. If there was a pivotal moment, Angie remembers it as just before Easter when we played a series against Korea. She remembers me asking her if she wanted to go to the Olympics. Her affirmative grunt was followed by me saying, 'If you keep playing as you are, you can make it.'

By the end of July, Angie was still improving and her form was emphatic enough for her to be a real chance. We had given her responsibility to run out on defensive corners and that, she felt, gave her the confidence that she was needed by the team. When we got on the plane to fly to Sydney, Angie finally believed it would happen. It had become real.

While the Olympic tournament was partly a blur to Angie, she remembers feeling self-contained in that her job was well circumscribed and clearly defined. That helped her focus on the task and feel able to contribute.

Perhaps the most important part of Angie's story is that from the time of her introduction to the team to becoming an Olympic gold medallist, a period of almost two years, she had doubts that she was good enough to make it. As coaches, we tried to grade her introduction with appropriate expectations at every stage until she was ready to handle it all. Along the way Angie's doubts were eased especially by Jenny Morris and Renita Garard. These two senior players may or may not have known what Angie could add to the team. Yet they helped her believe that she could make the team. Both had their own doubts about selection yet they were willing to assist their young team-mate make her way. That is real altruism in action.

Whatever the circumstances, I believe teams and organisations ignore youth at their peril. Young pretenders, managed well, lift the attitude, tone and output of any organisation, for

> **Young pretenders, managed well, lift the attitude, tone and output of any organisation, for they challenge orthodoxy and embrace and introduce change and new ideas almost unconsciously.**

they challenge orthodoxy and embrace and introduce change and new ideas almost unconsciously. Equally, they cause senior players to examine their own motives and often bring out cases of selflessness that can only benefit the group. Team members who focus on young pretenders because they fear losing their spot usually do. Those who seek to improve the team by promoting new talent also usually achieve their aim!

Be leaderful

During the last two years of our program, we broke down the previously hierarchical leadership structure of our group in an effort to get greater involvement from all our players. We achieved more interaction, and more involvement, within the group, but in my view we were only starting to see the sort of total involvement that may someday, somewhere be possible if the concept is taken further.

'Social loafing' occurs when group members shirk responsibility and sit on their hands when not in formal leadership roles. It is manifested in responses such as, 'I'm not responsible for that', which we commonly hear. By trying to build a 'leaderful' group in which interaction and curiosity and involvement are expected at every level, your organisation or team can be greatly refreshed. The introduction of youth is one method. Sharing leadership roles is another approach that refreshes the group.

I want athletes who challenge orthodoxy, are willing to speak their minds, put the group or team first, and set a tone and example that is

> **By trying to build a 'leaderful' group in which interaction and curiosity and involvement are expected at every level, your organisation or team can be greatly refreshed.**

uplifting and inclusive. These qualities are important for leaders and in my view the best teams have many such people, not just a designated leader. Those who are not curious or interested in the dynamic of the team are usually happy just to follow or drift. Vibrant, innovative and interactive groups do not have many such people.

In business as in sport the best teams and organisations are full of people who take responsibility for what happens and are continually trying to improve performance. Those that only do enough to stay out of trouble add little.

Some tips to refresh the team or organisation

1 Introduce new talent. New staff in an office can be as influential as new players in a team. Every new member changes the interactions and dynamics of the group. However, standards must be retained so it is important that good judgment is shown when new members are chosen. If someone is not up to the required standard, there is the danger of resentment. The reintroduction of a previously discarded player or worker can also refresh the group, albeit to a lesser extent than a new face.

2 Encourage lateral thinking – seek ideas from other sports or types of organisation, or from different fields of endeavour.

3 Change leadership structures or promotion processes or the way you prepare for matches or presentations. Altering any of the structures or processes of the team or workforce can help refresh the group. Rejigging leadership structures is especially interesting as it can prompt the most influential and persuasive team members to re-examine their motives.

4 New tactics and strategies, a new way of lining up, new names for positions and plays all serve to refresh the way the team sees itself. Similarly, the workplace can be refreshed even though there might not be great changes in personnel.

9 Avoid Recycling

Perhaps one of the most seductive tendencies in the successful organisation is to keep doing things the same way. After all, the methods are proven and achieved results last time, last week, last year or in recent memory.

After being successful in 1996 at the Atlanta Olympics, the Hockeyroos' approach to the task ahead was to look for ways of making our program better. We looked at every part of the program to find better ways to do things. This sort of examination should never be a matter of discarding everything (or nothing) but should entail a balance between retaining what is good and embellishing what can be improved.

Make a winning team better

Be wary of those whose approach is 'if it ain't broke, don't fix it'. Such an approach usually indicates arrogance, sloth or anxiety. None of these states is useful if you wish to stay at the top. Indeed, my experience is that it is a good idea to break down your organisation into its component parts and seek to introduce new ideas and methods in every area. One of the many myths of sport is a version of the 'if it ain't broke' approach – the 'never change a winning team' dictum. Of course you should always aim to improve a team, whether winning or losing. The same applies in business.

> **You should always aim to improve a team, whether winning or losing.**

Embrace change

The most important part of staying at the top is being able to embrace change. I have discussed renewing the team personnel and stimulating them by redefining challenges. The third element of embracing change is to renew the processes of your organisation. This is where we avoid recycling. This is where the methods and means of coaching your team or organisation are reviewed and renewed.

So we have refreshed 'who' we teach by introducing new people and challenging the comfortable older staff. Now we must look at 'how' we do 'what' we do.

During 1997 and 1998, we changed the structure of the Hockeyroos' game and our general tactical approach. Because of rule changes – offside was removed in 1997 – this process was expanded as we experimented with and discovered new ways of countering opponents in an offside-free game. We collected and analysed new and more searching statistics to enable us to look behind our results. To do this, we introduced new staff with new ideas and skills, and embraced new technology. The sophistication of this digital age has made for great progress in analysing sports performance.

While some core principles remained in our preparation and were strengthened, there was considerable change. Usually elements and components evolve within any program and ours was no different. For instance, we had introduced yoga to the group in 1996. By 2000, we were still using it to ensure flexibility, discipline and good body awareness, but in quite a different way. Similarly, during the Sydney Olympiad, we extensively renovated the way the Hockeyroos analysed the game statistically. By doing so, we provided more useful information for the athletes and gained a much better way of analysing strengths and weaknesses. Changes need not be huge or dramatic. Rather they should be part of a continuously evolving scene.

In Olympic sports these overall reviews tend

to occur every four years with coaching appointments or rule changes. My experience in football tells me that they also occur with new coaching appointments.

For business such leadership shifts clearly define times for introspection and analysis. However, it would seem that such a process should be part of the regular renewal and review within an efficient and progressive organisation. Some businesses will have the vibrance to do this within their structure. Others may require the catalyst of outside consultants or experts to undertake such internal searching. However it is done it needs to intimately involve the ideas and suggestions of those working in the organisation. Their response to renewal opportunities and change will tell the managers much about them and the business!

Changes need not be huge or dramatic. Rather they should be part of a continuously evolving scene.

Change comes from within as well as without

In sport, elite athletes are at the cutting edge of innovation when it comes to technique and skill. Often new ways of doing things are invented by the athletes as they explore the game's techniques. This can occur at practice or during matches. Indeed, it was my experience as a player that quite regularly I would spontaneously do something different or new that surprised me.

As a coach, every year I would see players exhibit new skills that had not been part of the game a few years ago. Managers should listen to, engage and watch employees as they will often renew processes without any input from above. When such help comes your way recognise it, reward it and use it.

> **The best organisations encourage difference and enthusiastic contributions to the program.**

Part of avoiding recycling is embodied in the ability to accept and acknowledge differences. This approach encourages participants and stakeholders to make suggestions and to challenge orthodoxy. Most of us can accept our suggestions not being adopted or introduced every time, but we do expect debate and consideration. The best organisations encourage difference and enthusiastic contributions to the program. Such an approach stimulates change, innovation and experimentation. It is this that helps us stay at the top.

Some tips to avoid recycling

1 Never give any credence to the 'if it ain't broke, don't fix it' approach.

2 Always try to improve a winning team.

3 Listen to staff, employees or athletes. Encourage them to put forward suggestions and make recommendations. Implement a system whereby all ideas get sympathetic hearings.

4 Embrace new technology and any advances it might bring.

5 Measure performance in new ways. Using objective data to evaluate performance can be really useful. We all need reality checks from time to time.

6 Experiment with the best of your new ideas. Don't be afraid to take risks that are calculated.

7 If you experiment and take risks, you will find other teams and organisations may overreact, and will find it harder to read your game or strategy. Even if the strategy doesn't work or is eventually rejected your opponents are often put off balance by the experimental process. If it causes you to temporarily fail it may make them overconfident. Again a good thing!

8 Don't apologise for change.

9 Don't change for change's sake. Much that you are doing must be good, otherwise you wouldn't be at the top. Assess carefully the practices and personnel that require attention.

10 Review every process in the organisation, looking for more efficiency, better quality and more depth and flexibility.

11 Remember, 'more' isn't necessarily 'better'. The goal is always better quality whatever the changes.

10 Face Your Foes

What sorts of things can cause us to lose our way once we have tasted success? In general terms, most of us would identify complacency as something that distracts us or slows us down in our productivity or energy. Complacency is sometimes manifested, somewhat surprisingly, as overconfidence, or it might show up as failure to acknowledge how we managed to be good in the past. Once you start to lose awareness of the practices and behaviours that underpin your success, your performance and consistency will slip as those practices and behaviours diminish or are lost. Let's look now at some more specific foes, including some that disguise themselves at times as complacency.

Acceptance: it's someone else's turn

The most insidious of foes is acceptance. This enemy is always about once your team or organisation has managed to reach the top. There is a little voice inside you that tells you it is someone else's turn. You have had your moment in the sun and now the pendulum will swing towards the next team, group, person or organisation, which by some benevolent power will now have their 'turn'.

> **Once you start to lose awareness of the practices and behaviours that underpin your success, your performance and consistency will slip as those practices and behaviours diminish or are lost.**

This orthodoxy is oft repeated and believed by many. It serves often as a convenient rationalisation for those who have let their standards slip. Similarly, for those who are endeavouring to take the champion's place at the top, it is comforting to think that it will soon be their turn, that the wheel of fortune will swing in their favour.

All this is arrant nonsense. It is never your turn to win the gold medal at the Olympics. Even the most remarkable and fortuitous victory can be explained by objective measures rather than by 'your turn' coming up. Steven Bradbury's gold medal in speed skating in 2002 at the Salt Lake City Winter Olympics was incredibly lucky in a sport that is structured in a way that allows such possibilities to occur. This could not happen in the 100 metres at the summer Olympics. In my view that is one of the weaknesses of the speed-skating discipline. Bradbury was exceedingly fortunate on consecutive occasions, but that does not mean it was his turn to win. It was just an isolated freak occurrence.

You do not go about preparing to be a world champion by hoping for a freak sequence of lucky breaks. What you must do is pay attention to the details, work diligently at your skills, physical capacities, strategy and mental disciplines and you then give yourself a chance if you already have some exceptional natural gifts. It is never anyone's turn to win the gold medal; it must be earned. Notwithstanding occasional aberrations, the means to win gold is within the grasp of anyone who is already a champion.

Whether seeking a second gold medal or another year of growth in our business, we need to be aware of the undermining foe of acceptance. It is nobody else's turn to be the best unless you

---

It is never anyone's turn to win the gold medal; it must be earned.

---

let your standards slip, lose focus on the values that made you great and stop learning and growing as an athlete or organisation. Taking calculated risks, seeking new solutions, embracing new technology and training methods and continuing to work at your game or business are the things that starve the bogey of acceptance.

Elite performers should be aware that acceptance will come knocking. It will offer a rationale for slipping standards and tell you it's not your fault if things don't work out. Those who want to stay on top know this foe. They expect it to visit and they slam the door on it as they get on with the practices and behaviours that made them champions in the first place.

Expectation: it'll be okay on the day

The converse of acceptance is the folly of expectation. While part of you might be suggesting it is someone else's turn, there is another part (which has experienced success before) saying, 'Don't worry, it will be okay on the day.' This is yet another manifestation of complacency. Expectation can be reassuring, and because in the past things have worked on the day we start to think that it will be the same again.

My experience as a player at the elite level in major competitions was disappointing: only three wins in eight 'must win' matches. That experience underpinned my fervent desire as a coach to always be well prepared and never to think things would be okay on the day. Even with the best preparation, the best players and the best strategy, things can go wrong on the day.

Teams and organisations need to be prepared for the problems and the difficulties that can bring them undone. You must prepare diligently

> **Even with the best preparation, the best players and the best strategy, things can go wrong on the day.**

for the contests ahead and have strategies for handling every possibility. The Hockeyroos developed a 'situation index' that gave us a plan for dealing with all the problems that we knew could arise in a contest.

Perhaps the best antidote for the delusion that it will be okay on the day is the experience of failure. A few losses or setbacks can quickly sharpen your focus on the task ahead. Complacency and blind faith are replaced by the more urgent desire to rediscover what it was that underpinned our success. We all tend to forget the trials and tribulations that forged our path to the top. Over time, past successes come to seem as almost inevitable. Teams that have won rarely analyse the game as closely as the teams that lost. Losses and setbacks are useful reminders of what is required to be the best. Failures or disappointments can also remind us of how much we enjoy success and want to maintain it.

Doubts: am I good enough?

Doubts can be a positive thing, by making us acutely aware of the need to work hard and follow our first five principles, but they can act negatively, by eroding our confidence and dragging us into lethargy and inactivity.

As ever, Shakespeare got it right, this time in *Measure for Measure*: 'Our doubts are traitors and makes us lose the good we oft might win by fearing to attempt . . .' We can be paralysed by doubts and uncertainty. Tolstoy put it another way in his short story 'Father Serquis': 'When he banished doubt, he also banished desire.' We need enough doubt to keep our engine running and to keep us inquisitive, but too much doubt can paralyse us.

> **Losses and setbacks are useful reminders of what is required to be the best.**

One of the greatest mistakes that an athlete in a complex team game can make is to be indecisive. It is often far better to be decisive and not choose the best option, than to dither and delay, as the best option chosen too late will no longer be the best option. Indeed, it can suddenly become the worst option, because if the opponents are any good it will be the option that they cover first.

It is crucial that we acknowledge our doubts and learn how to respond to them if we wish to perform at our best. The optimal state of doubt is one in which the opposition is respected, but not feared. Too much anxiety can paralyse our capacity to perform yet an appropriate respect for our opponent can stimulate us to be vigilant, sharp and to prepare fully.

> **The optimal state of doubt is one in which the opposition is respected, but not feared.**

Herb Elliot is acknowledged as Australia's premier male track athlete of the twentieth century. Unbeaten in forty-four races in the 1500 metres and the mile, he said his apprehensions fuelled his capacity to train hard and to compete at the elite level. Optimal performance requires acknowledgment of the possibility of failure and the mental capacity to deal with it. At times both desire to succeed and concern about not performing form part of the spectrum of emotion that athletes, coaches, managers and anyone trying to be the best must manage.

Every one of us knows about performance anxiety. Many times in the course of your life you will ask yourself: 'Am I good enough?', 'Am I well prepared?', 'Will we be able to prevail?', 'Have we worked hard enough?'. Those who practise excellence, prepare thoroughly, learn from every source, work co-operatively and are resilient and flexible will be able to manage doubt and fear and use them productively to reach optimal alertness.

The athlete, team or organisation that has already achieved success should not have more of an issue with doubt than those still trying to build success, yet often doubts are highlighted by the glare of publicity and expectation that goes with champion status. Leading into the Sydney Olympics, the Hockeyroos were in just such a spotlight of expectation. Players were scrutinised and analysed and accordingly felt significant pressure over and above the pressure that each individual had to wrestle with every day. While within our group the pressure was manageable and could be diluted amongst the players, I believe for someone like Cathy Freeman this level of intensity must have been

> **Those who practise excellence, prepare thoroughly, learn from every source, work co-operatively and are resilient and flexible will be able to manage doubt and fear.**

almost unbearable. That she came through it so well is a testimony not only to her resilience and quality as an athlete, but also to the quality of her preparation.

Some tips for facing your foes

1 Know that they come from within. In sport and business many of the greatest threats to performance come from within rather than without. The physical presence of your opponents or competition is what you prepare for and can deal with if prepared. However, the mental battles are often much more difficult to win.

Teams lose the big matches for a variety of reasons, but many of them can be found within the minds of the players and have nothing to do with their physical ability.

Here are a few common reasons:

- Sometimes teams play conservatively because they are afraid to take risks or make mistakes – that's fatal.

- Sometimes they expect it'll be okay on the day, and when things go wrong they cannot cope with the thought they may lose – and therefore cannot recover. When teams or companies have a temporary setback in a game or presentation and slip into acceptance mode – it's someone else's turn.

- Sometimes this mindset even occurs before the game or when competition has begun. Teams are happy just to be in the final – that's all they hoped for. Companies are overjoyed to have been invited to make a bid or presentation. That's enough to make them happy! If you think that way, of course you are right – you won't go any further!

- Sometimes they get right ahead of themselves and even before the game has begun get absorbed in imagining their success. This can also fatally occur in a game when leading and players get distracted thinking about the outcome while their attention should still be on the process.

2 Try to be objective about everything you do so doubts don't take over. Your training and preparation should give you belief. Know too that

your opponents have weaknesses and
vulnerabilities.

3 Learn as much as possible about the
competition – you'll find they are fallible, human
and have faults. They will make mistakes if you
can apply pressure by doing your bit right.

4 Be open about the foes that can be your pitfalls.
Frank discussion of these issues will help you
devise strategies for coping with and handling
them when they arise.

Afterword

I think one of my greatest strengths is that I am curious about the world, how it works and why people do what they do. I am constantly looking to discover what it is that makes things happen as they do. There never seem to be enough hours in the day to cram in all the things I'd like to do. Most nights I go to bed having left much undone. I suspect I will always be this way.

This book is an attempt to crystallise my thoughts on what it takes to realise your potential – to be the best you can be, and then maintain that standard. Whether the enterprise is to maximise the quality of your family life, your business or your sporting team, there are ideas and directions within these pages that can help you achieve your aims.

I have not spent time talking about goal-setting because I was never someone who set long-term goals; rather I absorbed myself in my passions and allowed the outcome to evolve. This is not to say I think goal-setting is not important, only that for each of us it will assume a different value. Of course we all need to know where we are heading – just don't expect any fine detail when it comes to how things will work out.

I was always very clear about where I might end up and what I might achieve. As a child I indulged my dreams daily as I imagined myself representing my country in sport or as a doctor discovering a cure for disease. As an adult such

> **We all need to know where we are heading – just don't expect any fine detail when it comes to how things will work out.**

imaginings still form an important part of my expectations of myself and others.

During the year before the Sydney Olympics I regularly imagined what it would be like for the Hockeyroos to win, and mentally rehearsed much of what would go into being successful. Hundreds of scenarios came into my mind as the year progressed. Very often these imaginings were converted into concrete ideas that found expression in our training and play.

I have always maintained that coaches who can predict what will happen in a game are either very gifted or just kidding themselves. I always knew what my team could do, but I could never be sure they would be able to reproduce it in the competitive environment of the game. Similarly, in business it would seem that you can only outline a strategy and hope your employees will put it into effect with diligence. You can never be sure about the competition, but a thorough knowledge of their past record and behaviours will help.

What I think is true is that your preparation and thoroughness in building your team or business give you the best chance of success. Mostly, if you pay attention to thoroughness in the areas I have outlined you will perform close to your potential. Certainly if you don't have good people, well trained, working together and resilient you will struggle.

Central to doing this is not only knowing what to do and who should do it, but also knowing yourself. For it is our personality – both strengths and weaknesses – that we take with us into any enterprise. Just as the personality of the players impinges on their performance, so does that of management.

I have not offered a template for success in

> **What I think is true is that your preparation and thoroughness in building your team or business give you the best chance of success.**

these pages; rather I suggest a pathway or at least offer some ideas that may help you cobble together your own path.

I am reputed to be stubborn, argumentative and, at times, singleminded and self-centred to the point of rudeness. I suspect these criticisms are fair. Yet these faults are balanced by a directness that can clarify issues, the ability to see the other side (not always immediately, I admit) and a certain perseverance in the face of disappointment. When managing people it is important to know your own perspectives and foibles as well as to try to understand the point of view of others.

I find it difficult to see how people can be extremely certain about things, and this is what I

When managing people it is important to know your own perspectives and foibles as well as to try to understand the point of view of others.

---

believe makes me argumentative. Metaphysical certainty (such as belief in God) really puzzles me, yet I can see the attraction to the arguments for some great design. Mostly though, I suppose all we can hope for is to do the best possible job with the gifts we are given, and to make a difference to those around us that improves their lives. In writing this book, I hope in some small way to do that!

Richard Charlesworth

The Coach: Managing for Success

Ric Charlesworth confirmed his place as Australia's most successful coach after steering the Hockeyroos to back-to-back gold medal victories at the Atlanta and Sydney Olympics.

Taking the Hockeyroos' triumph at the 2000 Games as his starting point, Ric offers fascinating and useful insights into his innovative coaching philosophies. These ideas can be applied within and outside the sporting world to achieve success. His theories about co-operation and striving for excellence can be used by managers, business people and everyone who is working to reach a goal.

'*The Coach* takes you inside Ric's sports world. It's fascinating, extremely well planned and thought provoking – but then that is Ric's way. A must read for players and coaches regardless of your sport.'
WAYNE BENNETT, FIVE TIMES PREMIERSHIP COACH FOR THE BRISBANE BRONCOS

'My reading round sporting performance, and in particular coaching, has been prolific...But none in my opinion do it better than *The Coach*'
DAVID PARKIN, FOUR TIMES AFL PREMIERSHIP COACH

Shakespeare the Coach

A brilliant motivational handbook for coaches, managers, teachers and trainers that utilises Shakespeare's genius to get the most out of you and your team's performance.

Ric Charlesworth, world-champion coach and bestselling author of *The Coach: Managing for Success and Staying at the Top,* has long been an ardent fan of William Shakespeare's plays and poetry. Over the course of a career that has seen Ric as medical graduate, Olympic sportsman, first-class cricketer, politician and champion coach, he has observed many of his own thoughts on coaching and people management mirrored by Shakespeare the Coach. Ric combines forces with Shakespeare to produce a blueprint for every manager, coach, team leader or anyone motivated to achieve, that will allow them to harness their potential.

Quirky, learned, fascinating and full of deep wisdom, Shakespeare the Coach is a fresh approach to achieve your maximum performance.